Advance Praise

The beauty of Wendy's book is its simplicity. Even after having worked with her, reading this reminded me of why being organized is so important. I encourage you to not only read it, but take action and implement her systems. They are that easy! No more stacks of papers on your desk or wondering where you put that important document. Every piece of information has its place and you will know where everything is. I use Wendy's strategies daily and I am considerably more productive and much less stressed. Having an organized work life is simply priceless.

Eric Griffin/Super Cuts

As someone who has spent 20 years running a successful work-from-home, creative, video and marketing agency while raising two kids in spite of being an organizationally-challenged, multi-tasking procrastinator—not because of it— Wendy Ellin's take-no-prisoners approach is just what I needed to take my business and my life to a more orderly and satisfying place. Enough Is Enough, Get Control of Your Stuff! is an easy to follow guide for achieving your goals, streamlining your priorities and as she says, "getting more **life** *out of life." I'd highly recommend this book for those—like me—who are looking at ways to "reinvent" themselves for the second half of life.*

Susan Heller Shoer/President & Creative Director, Creative Word & Image, Inc.

Organization is the key to my sanity. Wendy's book, Enough Is Enough, Get Control of Your Stuff! *offers easy solutions with step-by-step instructions that will enable you to remain in the land of the sane. I have attended Wendy's seminars in the past and I always leave wishing I could take her home with me. Now I can with this wonderfully written book! She writes like she speaks—logical, concise and no-nonsense. I will highly recommend this book to everyone I know.*

Kellyann Dunning/Membership Director, The Buckhead Club

Enough Is Enough,
Get Control of Your Stuff!

Simple, street-smart PRODUCTIVITY TOOLS & TECHNIQUES to help you close the gap between where you are and where you want to be in your business and in your life.

Wendy.

WENDY ELLIN

BOOKLOGIX®
Alpharetta, Georgia

ISBN: 978-1-61005-567-3

This book may be purchased in bulk for educational, business, fundraising or sales promotional use. For information please contact:
Wendy Ellin, wendy@wendyellin.com
www.wendyellin.com

☻ This paper meets the requirements of ANSI/NISO Z39.48-1992 (Permanence of Paper)

Cover and interior layout design by: Vanessa Lowry

Table of Contents

Foreword

We all frequently face major choice-points in our lives. Moments in time when we say yes, or no, to a potential life-changing idea or option. Years ago I was minding my own business while leisurely reading a book by the late Charlie "T" Jones when my eyes passed over the following sentence: "You will be the same person in five years as you are today except for the people you meet and the books you read."

This simple statement turned out to be the genesis of a major choice-point for me. I decided that forevermore my response to frustration, chaos, or any form of less-than-desirable circumstances in my life would be to seek an author who offered ideas and solutions to make the less-than-desirable circumstances go away. This choice has, and continues, to serve me quite well.

Why don't you join me? Make a similar decision and read Wendy's book. It basically offers very simple ideas for converting chaos to order in your life. Think about it. How much would a little more order and serenity be worth to you right now? How about a little more quality time with friends, family, and others important to you...or perhaps even more quality time with important work projects? I suspect for most of you, these things would be worth a lot.

We live in a world that encourages chaos. That is the default mode for most people nowadays. But don't buy into the illusion that that is "just the way things are." Read this book, make the choice to try Wendy's ideas and step out of the madness that so many people seem ever-so-willing to tolerate.

If you currently feel centered and grounded and are enjoying plenty of quality moments in your life, congratulations—you have avoided the trap that has snared many in our chaotic society. If this is not the case, you are at a choice-point. Choose a new lifestyle; begin this choice by simply reading and trying the ideas in *Enough Is Enough, Get Control of Your Stuff!*

Chris Crouch
President
DME Training & Consulting

Preface

I would like to dedicate this book to my Advisory Board, the four people in my life without whose lessons I would not have taken this path I have chosen. All four of these men have advised me, taught me, mentored me and inspired me to give to the world all that I have in the most honest, authentic, and joyful way possible.

My father, Jim Rogers, who showed me many years ago that choosing to live the life you were meant to live, no matter what others may think or say, is the only way to live. Sometimes you don't know that until many years later, as was the case for me. But when you do finally discover what that path looks like, the road is as clear as the light of day.

To my cousin Stevie Kaufman, who also taught me that being unique and authentic in this world is something to not only be proud of, but ultimately the only way to truly enjoy every minute of every day you are alive. He lived his shortened life out loud with truth, humor, talent, friendship, love, humility, and grace right until the very end. For this, and for the love and friendship we shared, I am eternally grateful.

To my father-in-law Lester Ellin, you are the one who, right from the beginning, saw something in me and blessed my ideas and inspiration for leaving the corporate world and finding my life's work. Thank you for believing in, and encouraging me to harness my natural abilities and interests to help the world be a better (or at least happier) place to be. Although our time together was short, it was nothing short of respectful for a man who showed me how hard work and commitment could take you places you never thought you'd see.

And lastly, but most importantly, to my pop-pop Mickey Behrend. You are the man I looked up to the most. You are the one who first defined and refined the words character, integrity, and success. Your passion for life, humor, and drive for success were powerful messages you shared with me since the day I was old enough to understand. You loved me and showed me love all the days of our lives together, and it is from that unconditional love and support that you inspired me to be the best I can be while enjoying each and every moment.

Thank you all for continuing to see me through this incredible journey.

When you know better, you do better.

Maya Angelou

INTRODUCTION
Moving With Momentum

I've never written a book. But then again, I never thought I had anything to share until I *looked* at how much I had to share. Ever since launching my business in 2000, it has become clearer to me that there is a direct correlation between how I live my life and the daily joy I experience. Okay, so not every day is as joyous as others, but for the most part, I experience my life with joy, positivity, low stress, and an overall sense of peace of mind.

What that means is that although I may be crazy busy all the time (or at least it certainly feels that way), all the facets of my life that are important to me are moving with ***momentum***—that is, positive movement forward while offering and maintaining balance. My life feels like a "well-oiled machine"—each wheel cranking at its own steady pace while supporting the other wheels as they do the same. What it also means is that, when I turn the light out at night, my head "turns off" as well. I'm not lying there wondering what I didn't get done or what may have fallen through the cracks today, or stressing out about what I have to do tomorrow. I've got control over my life and what I have to do, and I comfortably slide into slumber, knowing it will all get done when it should.

The facets that I speak of are my marriage, my family, my business, my physical and mental health & wellness, my spiritual practice, and my relationships. Each one of these gets the attention it needs to continue growing me as a spouse, a step-mom, a business coach and consultant, a healthy person, a spiritual being, and a friend. Sometimes I focus more heavily on one or two facets based on what is going on for me at any particular time, but rarely is any one part of my life being neglected due to focusing on something else.

It's not uncommon for us women to spend a good part of our time trying to be everything to everybody. It's all about how much we can get done, who we can please and attend to, and what, if anything, is left for ourselves when all is said and done.

This book is to provide you with my "nuts & bolts" for living your life in a way that works—no matter what that looks like for you. It is designed to invite you to make more sense of your life—particularly if the way you are living isn't satisfying you. It speaks to those who see the value in learning solutions that are relatable, flexible, adaptable, and simple. Nothing more, nothing less. Oh yes, there is one more thing...powerful results if you stick with it long enough!

Whether it's the corporate ladder you are climbing, the new business you are building, or the stay-more-often-at-home mom you are desiring to be, having simple systems for getting control of your time and your daily life are essential to succeeding with efficiency, energy, balance, and joy.

My husband, Marty, once commented years ago, "You're just organized because you're too lazy to look for things." Really? While laughing, I was quickly back at him with, "No—I actually don't see *THE POINT* in looking for things!"

It ultimately has to come down to **what works for you!** Do you like where you are, or the direction in which you are headed? Great! Sustain it, embrace it, enjoy it! But if you do not like where you are, or where you're headed—here comes good news—you can change the direction you are going anytime you choose! Where you are now is just a stop along your journey. And within each step comes the discovery that new paths are available to you and once chosen, can significantly enhance the power and possibilities in your life's experience.

Real Momentum Moment

I am currently coaching a client who, when asked "What are your reasons for wanting this coaching?" responded, "To help regain commitment, discipline, and add pizzazz back into my life." Now that's an emphatic "Why" I can truly support!

I hope to make that connection with you—to hit a nerve. To awaken you to the possibility that being organized, adopting good organizational skills, and staying engaged in this habit-changing process is not nearly as difficult as you think. Starting today, you can choose to live differently to create new daily routines that will motivate you to get out of bed every morning with energy and passion for what you do. And to ensure that when you turn the lights out at night, your head "turns off" as well.

Thanks for keeping an open mind. And for embracing the notion that sometimes it's not the "**what** to do," but the "**how** to do" that makes the difference.

Make Your Move Toward Momentum Intro

Spend a few minutes writing down your reasons for changing the way you live. What would doing things differently look like? What's not working that you think having a new system for living your life would fix? What's in it for you? Why change your daily habits around how your environment functions?

*It's the power of the **Why?** that directly affects the outcome of the challenge! Make sure your reason or reasons hold so much value for you that there is no turning back until it's your new reality.*

*We were not meant
to be perfect,
we were meant
to be whole.*

Jane Fonda

Things do not change,
we change.

Henry David Thoreau

CHAPTER 1

Keeping Your Head in the Game

Over the past several years, I have become increasingly interested in The Law of Attraction. It started when the internet movie The Secret, created by Rhonda Byrne, came out and helped me hone in on my true belief— that what you focus on expands. That's my simplest explanation for the way that law works in the universe. Up until then, I had not thought of myself as a particularly spiritual person, but when I spent some time listening and learning from various educational entities, I "got it." I got that whatever kind of energy you put out into the universe is what comes back to you; that our actions are not actions until they are first thoughts; that we can be active in shaping those thoughts, and therefore the actions that spring from them. So I started to look at what I do in this world to combine the teachings of The Law of Attraction with the tools necessary for changing habits. Because after all, isn't changing unsuccessful habits what we are ultimately talking about here?

So with that in mind, it is imperative to "keep your head in the game" when talking about changing the way you live to get different results. One of the ways I frequently describe what I do to others is…

"I am the **Weight Watchers** and the **SmokEnders** of **Getting Organized.**"

What does that mean? Well, for starters, what losing weight, quitting smoking, and getting organized all have in common is that they are the top three New Year's Resolutions. Each one involves changing habits for one reason or another, to get different results that ultimately IMPACT YOUR LIFE IN A POSITIVE WAY.

And what all three also have in common is that whether you are trying to lose weight, quit smoking or get organized, there are five key ingredients necessary for success.

1. Commitment
2. Dedication
3. Perseverance
4. Determination
5. A system or process

It takes a carefully considered process, commitment to the changes that the process will demand, dedication to the reality that no habit change comes overnight, perseverance in the direction of your choice, and focused determination to see you through to your goal.

Choosing vs. Wanting

Let's take losing weight. When I am speaking to a crowd of either ten or 1,000 and I ask, "By a show of hands, how many of you would like to lose weight?" more than half the room raises their hand. No exception, every time. That is not surprising, as a good percentage of our society is not happy with their weight for one reason or another. But when I follow that question with, "By a show of hands, how many of you ARE NOW READY TO *CHOOSE* to lose weight?" the number of raised hands diminishes substantially. Yes, every time, no exception. (At least the ones that do not raise their hands the second time are honest that they do not have the requisite serious mental intent, the attitude that can support change. I give them credit for knowing themselves!)

Most of the people who are willing to say out loud, to me and to their colleagues or even to strangers, that the time is now to get started, have reached a critical understanding: habit change MUST start inside your head, with the strong support of your heart. No external pressure is enough, no product is enough, no promise is enough—until the click inside the head switches to "Yes!" The ones that choose to lose the weight are those that *get it*; that it starts first in your head before your body. It's because their "why?" for choosing to tackle something tough is so clear, bold, loud, red, and flashing in front of them that they have actually built up excitement around the process. They actually can't wait to start!

I am lucky—I have real discipline, and I happen to LOVE CHANGE! I don't know where it comes from—most likely from not liking something and wanting the different outcome so badly that nothing stops me until I get it. I see the value in the changes I make—the reward is either big enough, healthy enough, and/or sometimes even smart enough. Like quitting smoking. I smoked cigarettes for sixteen years. Every time someone asked me to quit, I'd go out and smoke two. The more someone nagged me about it, the more I smoked. It wasn't about anyone else wanting me to quit—that's way too hard a habit to change for anyone else but yourself. I finally got that I did not want to be a smoker anymore; I didn't want to be the only one who left a restaurant after dinner to go outside for a smoke; I did not want my clothes smelling like smoke; and I was sick of making cigarettes and coffee a meal replacement. So, now finally being committed to change for me, I went to SmokEnders and learned how to wean myself off of them until there was no reason to smoke anymore. Presented with a carefully considered system, I was committed, dedicated and determined, and I persevered. And it worked. I'm thankful on so many levels, including—and most importantly—my health.

And speaking of health, it is one of the driving factors in all three resolutions we speak of. In losing weight and quitting smoking, the positive health attributes are obvious. Getting organized and productive has just as many positive health ramifications that not only affect your physical health, but affect your mental health as well. Low stress, increased joy, and peace of mind are just a few of the benefits derived from changing this habit.

Remember, shining a light on something doesn't make it go away. It's ACTION = MOVEMENT = MOMENTUM that starts the process in the right direction.

So back to that system or process. We all know that when it comes to weight loss, there are an unlimited number of programs you can join to lose weight. But we also know that the better systems speak to more than what you put in your mouth. They also speak forcefully to the commitment of exercise; water intake; the proper amount of sleep; sticking to the program; and setting yourself up for new eating habits by ridding your pantry of unhealthy, tempting products. These all play a roll in the process of losing and keeping weight off.

The same goes for getting organized and productive. It's not just about a filing system or a neat and tidy desk. There are also the mental parts of changing daily habits; the de-cluttering process; the setting up new systems; the tweaking things to work for your specific situation; the element of time management; the issues of focusing and multi-tasking; the self-defeating behaviors like procrastination and perfectionism—all of these are related to this topic. Over the next several chapters, we are going to uncover simple steps for not only getting a handle on the process, but also for dealing with it all in a realistic, flexible way that will encourage you to hang in there long enough to reap the benefits.

So stick with me here. Each chapter has at least a few "nuts & bolts" that will help you build not only your new life, but also the momentum that goes with it!

Real Momentum Moment

Eric, a Supercuts franchisee, was completely distracted from all that surrounded him in his office. He envisioned his space looking and functioning differently, but wasn't sure how to make that happen. And all his built-up clutter created great overwhelm and continued to deter him from even getting started. Once he learned how to keep his head in the game, and now having systems in place for processing his workload, he is pleasantly amazed at how easy it is to get to his work, complete it, move on to the next project, and ease into his evening with satisfaction and pride. I'd say that's a worthy goal, wouldn't you?

Make Your Move Toward Momentum #1

Every morning before you start your day, sit quietly for a few minutes and envision what that day will look like. Literally see yourself navigating through your day, moving from place to place, getting to your appointments on time (or a little early), connecting positively with people in person or on the phone, getting your work done, and arriving back home at the end of the day with a huge sense of accomplishment and satisfaction. You have a much better chance of what you envision actually happening if you do this rather than winging it and hoping it turns out this way. Remember, getting it in your HEAD first starts the ball rolling in that direction.

*Happiness is not a pursuit,
it's a choice.*

Nothing good comes out of creating a space that you or someone else doesn't feel welcome in.

George Clooney

CHAPTER 2
Creating Productive Spaces

Look around you. What do you see? Piles of paper stacked on every corner of your desk? Paper "fanned" on the floor of your office in rows like dominos? Client bucket folders stacked and stuffed on your bookshelves in between books that you hope to read and magazines you never will?

Do you have a garage that you can't fit a car in because of the bicycles, lawn mower, baby stroller, hockey sticks, and garden tools? What about your kitchen drawers? Have you designated one full drawer as your "electrical bin" where miscellaneous cords and plugs take up residence? Do you actually still own the equipment that goes with those cords?

Some of us "live above our means" spatially. That means you have more stuff than your actual house can effectively hold! Yes, we don't only "live above our means" financially, but spatially as well.

So here's my theory about this…I'm fifty-five years old, and like everyone else, have been collecting stuff throughout my entire life. Fifty-five years' worth of stuff—you can imagine how much that is! I'm a very healthy fifty-five-year-old. I eat carefully, exercise regularly, and do what it takes to keep my mental health intact. So given this, I may have the chance to live at least another thirty-five years, and maybe more. Therefore, if I don't get rid of some of what I've collected over the past fifty-five years, where will I put what's coming in over the next thirty-five? Make sense? Oh sure, you can certainly rent a unit from a storage facility each month to house the things that can't fit in your house. But most likely, that's the stuff that you never even go visit in storage much less take out to get rid of. You see my point?

De-cluttering your life is a challenge I invite you to consider. If you don't use it, need it, or love it—LET IT GO! It sounds simple, but not so for some. Enlist a spouse, child, or friend dedicated to thinning out your possessions, or seek professional help if you can't do it alone.

When I talk about clutter, I am less concerned with how it looks and more concerned with **HOW YOUR ENVIRONMENT FUNCTIONS**. If the clutter and disarray don't affect how you live, then continue to live that way. I am always focused on what doesn't work—because "if it isn't broken, don't fix it." So many people spend so much time looking for things—(sometimes things they just purchased literally two hours ago and can't seem to put their hands on)—yet they don't realize that it is the way they are living that isn't serving them well. They are reprinting documents they just printed three minutes ago that they can't locate. They have neither a system for where things go when they come in, nor routines for processing items on a daily basis. Things don't have a "permanent home" in their house, so it's easy to see how clutter can build. And just a small reminder... clutter may come into your life with little effort on your part, but it **will not** leave your life without some effort. That much I can promise!

Here's another way to look at clutter. I want you to imagine that your office is Philips Arena. That's where Bruce Springsteen would perform if he came to Atlanta; in New York, it would be Madison Square Garden; in Dallas, the American Airlines Center, in Denver, the Pepsi Center. You get the point—your office is an arena and your chair is the stage. So, imagine you are front and center (on stage) and you are trying to focus on what you are working on, yet all the stuff, the paper, the piles, the clutter surrounding you in your office are all raucous people—they are your audience. So tell me, do you have A FULL HOUSE? Because here is what is potentially happening…the pile on the far upper right corner of your desk, the one living in the "metal clutter holder" that you have is talking to you.

It's saying, "Hey you, don't forget about me, I'm due next Thursday at ten o'clock and you haven't touched me in weeks. Do you even remember I'm here?"

And the pile on the floor to the left of your desk is reminding you, "Hey buddy, you finished working on me three months ago and I'm still living on your floor over here, because you haven't found a permanent home for me yet."

And the stuff on the bookshelf is screaming…"What are you doing with me next? I'm the material for your nine o'clock conference call tomorrow morning."

Are you catching my drift? All the clutter in your office that surrounds you as you try to stay focused on the task at hand is talking to you—**ALL AT ONCE!** It is a serious distraction even if you are not aware that it is grabbing for your attention, but trust me, even if it is not actually crying out for your attention, you know it's there! You put it there hoping that it would remind you of something—you just can't figure out what! I'm not one of those people who declare that you should "only touch a piece of paper once." (The only pieces of paper I've ever recommended someone touch only once are Kleenex and toilet tissue!) My theory is to **ONLY TOUCH IT WHEN YOU NEED IT NEXT.** But like most people, you want to keep it "in sight" so that you don't forget to do it, yet if you keep everything in sight that you need to be reminded to do, the work staring at you becomes enough to send you right out the door to Starbucks, or better yet, into the bottomless pit of internet surfing. And that certainly doesn't aid the productive day you sought out to have.

So with all this "clutter talk" in mind, let's do something about it. Yes, we are going to start the de-clutter process by taking the following four steps:

1. Start in your office. Either at your business or home office, it doesn't matter. You'll potentially make the most impact there.

2. Grab some big plastic garbage bags or haul the company dumpster and recycle bin that reside in the copy room close to your office, but leave them outside the door to give yourself as much room as possible.

3. Make sure your phones are on "Forward" and your computer's "Out of Office Assistant" is on so you will not be disturbed. Start picking up one piece of paper at a time and determine whether to keep or toss. If you are tossing, have at it...right in the dumpster/recycle bin. If it's a keeper, put it aside in a box or basket and we'll talk about where it can go in Chapter 4. For now, this is the de-cluttering process where we are just making quick decisions to keep or toss.

4. If you don't <u>use it</u>, <u>need it</u> or <u>LOVE it</u>, strongly consider letting it go. And spend as little time as possible with "but what if I need it two months

or three years from now?" Most likely you can find it again. It's what got you in this mess to begin with—not being able to let it go because of the "what ifs" about it. It is, in fact, the day and age of Google so there are very few things you don't have access to. Have no fear, the internet is here…to stay!

(Let me please be clear that I am not suggesting you toss anything that you need to keep. I am just inviting you to start getting realistic about what you need and what you don't.)

Once you have done this process with every space that has you stuck in the downward spiral of clutter, you should be left with all the remaining papers, items, and keepsakes for which we will now find a permanent place.

The goal here is to create a space for yourself that makes you feel good...one that promotes productivity, creativity and passion—not stress, chaos, and dysfunction. It's one thing to do what you were put on this planet to do. It's another thing to do it in a way that serves you well, represents who you want to be in this universe and offers ongoing peace of mind.

Real Momentum Moment

After learning of my upcoming Productivity Workshop in her office, Cheryl A. with ACS tracked me down to inquire about how I could help her. When I first saw her double cubicle, my first thought was, Wow, she really could use my help, followed by I hope she has it in her! Because the more clutter and stuff, the bigger the challenge, but also the biggest reward. Let's just say that at the end of our eight hour session, not only was it an emotional experience we shared, but also a revealing one when she commented, "Now I can take a sick day."

To which I responded, "Really?"

"Yes, she said…before I couldn't take a sick day because I was afraid that no one would be able to find anything they need in my space in my absence." WOW, that was powerful. That is just who this woman is, always worrying about everyone else, but in this case finally taking care of herself at the same time.

Make Your Move Toward Momentum #2

*Put a date on the calendar **RIGHT NOW** for the de-cluttering session and follow the four steps for de-cluttering. Invite someone to join you who has your best interest at heart. Turn up the tunes and make this fun—you will be amazed at how enjoyable the purging process is once you get started. You'll let go of things you never thought you could part with—and before you know it, you'll feel lighter on your feet and the things that really matter will appear more clear and focused. Here's to your success!*

Change happens somewhere between the acceptance of now and the anticipation of what's to come.

Terri Trespicio

We are what we repeatedly do.
Therefore excellence
is not an act
but a habit.

Aristotle

CHAPTER 3

What's on Your Plate?

Remember in Chapter 1 I mentioned that sometimes it's not the "*what* to do" but the "*how* to do" that makes the difference? When it comes to systems for almost anything, I think the key to succeeding is the simplicity of the "*how.*" If what you are currently doing isn't working, offering a somewhat difficult or complicated alternative might just make matters worse. A new system or process should be simple and practical enough so that you stick with it long enough to reap the benefits. Research shows that it takes twenty-one days of repeated action for a habit to stick. The repeated action must be mentally and emotionally linked with "feeling right," which in turn encourages you to continue that action and adopt it as your new habit. So let's talk about the simplest solution possible for maximizing "right feelings" and establishing long-term results.

The system I use for getting control of my life is not something I invented. In fact, it's been around for decades and is shared and spoken about by many in the field of Professional Organizing. I call it my **COMMAND CENTRAL**. It's how I maintain **MOMENTUM** in my life, and I use it throughout each day. In its simplest form, it is referred to as the age-old "tickler system." It begins with having a file drawer or box to hang files in. Yes, that's right—those army green (not so attractive) hanging files we all use in offices around the world. We are going to start to make decisions with everything that comes into our lives—**WHEN IT COMES IN!** Having this system is a key to help make that happen.

So what are those things that come into your life that I'm speaking about? Well, for one, there's **PAPER**; lots of paper that comes in from all different directions. There's the mail that the mailman delivers to our mailbox. There's the memo that your assistant put in your inbox. There's the contract or policy change or update that is being passed around your team for your "read and sign" signature. Regardless of how badly you want to "go paperless," there will always be paper in your life! The sooner we face that fact and figure out what to do with it, the better off we will all be.

So let's continue...we next consider **VOICE MESSAGES**. Messages that we have waiting in our inbox either asking us, telling us or suggesting to us that we do something. And if nothing else, the "to do" that grabs our attention first is to return that call. Then there's the one that I devote an entire chapter to: **EMAIL.** I'll be brief here until we get to that chapter, but suffice it to say that it's become a bigger challenge and for some more of a problem than we ever expected. But it's one of the most popular, if not the fastest growing way in which we receive information. Oh yes, and **TEXT**—but that's a whole other story.

Then there are two (not as obvious) ways in which things find their way onto your "to do" list. One is **TO DO'S INITIATED BY SOMEONE ELSE**; someone stops you in the hallway of your business and asks you to do something for them—that's essentially an "incoming" item. And the last is **YOUR OWN RANDOM THOUGHTS**; as when you are driving home and at a red light, you remember that you have to call the pet sitter to reserve overnight care for the week you are going on vacation. These things happen more frequently than we expect or sometimes pay attention to, but they are equally as important as all the other "to do's" that enter our lives.

So now, the processing part! What if I told you that from this day forward, you were going to start processing everything that comes into your life (regardless of how it arrives) as it arrives? Don't freak out! It's much easier than you think. You see, one of the main problems with clutter is that things come into our lives in one of the six ways noted above, but since we have not created a processing system or a place for them to go, they don't go anywhere and ultimately form the piles you have in your office, on the kitchen counter, on your bedroom floor or elsewhere. So our goal is to create a place for what we are keeping so that we only have to put our hands on it when we need it next.

INTRODUCING THE *COMMAND CENTRAL* (CC)

If you are willing to let it, this Command Central System WILL CHANGE YOUR LIFE! Here's what you will need:

- A file box or desk drawer to house this system

- Three boxes of 25 hanging folders, (either letter or legal size, depending on the size of your file drawers)

- 3x5 cards

Now you are ready to start setting it up.

The system resembles the old-fashioned "tickler" system which requires:

- 31 hanging files with tabs numbered 1-31 on them;

- 12 hanging files with tabs labeled January through December; and

- 25 hanging folders left over to use when setting up your reference documents that you file alphabetically.

The basics are the 31 days of the month, the 12 months of the year, and the alphabetical reference folders. ***DOES IT GET ANY SIMPLER THAN THE DAYS OF THE MONTH, THE MONTHS OF THE YEAR, AND THE ABCs?***

At the end of this chapter, I have listed a website link for you to go to if you are interested in my tools associated with this system. But for now, each tab should have a number on it (1-31) or a month of the year (January-December). That would amount to forty-three hanging folders, plus the three "special" files I will share with you, totaling forty-six hanging folders in your Command Central drawer or file box. The remaining box of twenty-five folders should be set aside to create your alphabetical reference files for those documents you want to keep for future use.

There are also three additional special file tabs that I will walk you through.

Special File #1: **EASY ACCESS.** This is the very first file in your drawer before the number 1 file. It is where all the things live that you most frequently put your hands on and refer to. I have my passwords in that file so I don't have to look them up every time I can't remember one, which is often. I also put some "cheat" sheets I often use, like how to use FreeConferenceCall.com or the steps to downloading my camera to my computer. It's great for phone numbers you often use, internal phone extensions for employees, organizational charts, etc. I keep things that most people post on their corkboard in front of them (which is just another form of distraction to me) in this file. I don't want all that stuff in sight, but I still want it near me for easy access.

Special File #2: **PENDING RESPONSE (PR)**. This is a great file for housing all those things that you are waiting for from someone else—instead of them living in a pile on your desk or in your "metal clutter holder," they are in a file that is right behind Easy Access. I look at that file almost every day to see what is outstanding in the event it's been a few days and I may want to remind someone that I am waiting for their response. Again, this is a great file to have.

Special File#3: **RIP & READ.** This file ROCKS! You know all those magazines you have piling up against the wall in your office—high enough that they could serve as an end table—because you don't have time to look through, much less read them? Now, every time you get a magazine, give yourself twenty-four hours to go through it, rip out the articles you want to read, staple the corner, and pop them in your RIP & READ file for when you have time to read them. Then discard the magazine itself. Take the Rip & Read file with you when you travel. Arrive to an appointment early and read an article or two before the meeting starts. I never mind having to wait at a doctor's office because I look at it as built-in time to read from my R&R file—wouldn't you want to read something of your own choosing rather than some 1997 *Motor Trends* magazine with one-half the pages missing? Try that the next time you go to the doc's office—you'll be amazed at how less stressed you are about waiting!

Okay, so now that we have set up all the critical files that comprise your Command Central, you are ready to start processing what remains from the PURGING session I spoke of in Chapter 2. We are now going to give our attention to the box/basket into which you put all the things you really must keep and tackle—are you ready...? One piece of paper at a time!!

Wendy's Juicy Tidbit #1

Look at your business life like one big VOLLEYBALL GAME – your goal is to get as many balls out of your court and into someone else's every day, whether they come in by mail, email, text, voicemail, etc. It doesn't mean that they won't come back to you, but at least you are moving them out of "your court," which means productivity is happening.

FIVE STEPS FOR PROCESSING

Everything that comes into our lives falls into one of three categories. It's either something we need to take action on (Action Item); it's something we may want to refer to sometime in the future (Reference Item); or it's something that can be thrown away. If there is another category, I'm not aware of it. So we start by taking one of five steps to determine what happens with every single thing that comes your way.

1. **LET IT GO** – This is where you get rid of what you don't need, want, or love. Plain and simple…once you get the hang of it! So when something comes into your life, the first thing you are going to ask yourself is "Do I need to keep this?" As I've said before, I'm not suggesting you toss anything you truly need to keep. I just want you to start strengthening that "LETTING GO" muscle so that you are only left with what you want or need to keep. Make this your first, threshold decision: *do I really need to retain this?* Trust me, once you get good at "letting go," you will be amazed at how good it feels.

Assuming you do not throw it away, choose from the following four steps:

2. **LET IT GO TO SOMEONE ELSE** – For those of you who have others to whom you can delegate, rejoice in this option and set these items aside to put in your system after your sorting and discarding are done!

A note about delegating. For a long time, I had no one to delegate any of my work to, so this choice was not an option for me, and it may not be one for you. But if it is, start honing in on your delegating skills so that you can empower those who work with you and leave what is unquestionably your work to yourself. The key to effective delegating lies in one word: communication. Are you asking for what you need and are you in agreement as to when you will receive it? I am a firm believer that there can never be too much communication when it comes to asking someone to do something for you. And how you ask is as important as the task at hand. Know what you hope to accomplish and state that expectation in clear terms. Confirm that the delagatee knows what is expected of her/ him, and the timeframe for completion. The conversation between you and the delegatee should enhance your effectiveness, should accomplish the necessary task, and should promote real cooperation between you.

3. ***DO IT NOW*** – This is a great one! It's for all those things that come into your life that you can respond to in **TWO MINUTES OR LESS!** That's right, make it happen and get it off your plate. Unless you are going to do these things during the sort and file process, set these items aside to put in your system after you're done!

A note about doing it now. We will talk about this more in Chapter 4 when we tackle our email inbox. But for now, it's important to see this step as one that will quickly eliminate much of what is waiting for you to handle. Once it is handled, you will feel like you just completed the "quick weight loss" plan. It requires a trained eye and some serious focus to get in, respond in two minutes or less and move on, but this is a discipline well worth developing. This is actually my favorite processing step—it allows me to get in, get out, and get rid of. So for all those messages that you can return, all those emails you can respond to, all those requests you can process in two MINUTES OR LESS – as NIKE so aptly puts it…JUST DO IT! That means taking a break at intervals during your day to see how many of these you can get out of your inbox or out of your voicemail box.

4. ***File in FURTHER ACTION files*** – These are the files in your COMMAND CENTRAL SYSTEM – it's where all the items you need to take further action on go until you need to see them next.

A note on COMMAND CENTRAL SYSTEM FILES: At the point you begin sorting items into your Command Central Action Files, you'll need to decide whether you need each individual item during one of the days left in the current month (1-31) or in a future month (January – December).

For example, let's say you have a doctor's appointment next week on July 9. It's a new doctor and you haven't been there previously so they email you directions to their office. Print them out and put them in the "9" file in your Command Central. This way when July 8 rolls around, and you see on your calendar that your doctor's appointment is the next day, you will have the directions waiting for you in the next day's file. It sure beats having to scramble that morning to find the email with their directions, right? So why not file it when it comes in on the date when you need it? This system not only keeps you organized and on top of what you have going on in your world, it saves you loads of time in having to look for things that are important to your success.

Wendy's Juicy Tidbit #2

Distinguish between "where you go" and "what you do" on a daily basis. That means don't have your "to go's" and your "to do's" in the same place. My "to go's" go on my calendar because they relate to a specific time (i.e., lunch appointment, client meeting, conference call, doctor appointment, etc.) My "to do's" go in my Command Central in the day that I want to get started on a certain project, or when it is due, depending on how long it takes to complete. I put my appointments on my calendar and then anything, like directions to that appointment, go in my CC on the day of the appointment.

Another example...you make flight reservations for a trip you are taking in November, and it's July. Print out the electronic ticket and put that in your November file. You'll never need to search for it on your computer or wonder where that information is because as long as you remember that the trip is in November, you'll be able to find it. Or better yet, create a file folder with the name of the trip on the tab (i.e. Costa Rica 11/12) and everything including travel details goes in this folder and the folder lives in November. Then when it's November, take it and put it into the daily file for the day you are leaving. Make sense? I could go on and on with examples of what to put in this system, but I hope by now you get how this works.

This system allows you to plan ahead, so do just that. If you have a hard and fast deadline of next Friday, and the project takes a day or two to do, put those documents in the Wednesday before the deadline to give yourself the time you need to complete it. Always build in time for "unexpected interruptions"—the best way to handle them is…EXPECT THEM!

For those of you who would rather remain more electronic when it comes to processing your life, stay tuned. We will delve into that in **Chapter 4, Taming the Technology Tiger.**

5. ***File in FUTURE REFERENCE file*** – This is where all the things that you need to keep that are not action items live. Whether you need to refer to something once a year or once a week, it must have a permanent home in a Future Reference file. Otherwise, it will be living in a pile instead of a file, and that will only bring you right back to where you started, so let's not go there. I have a "Personal Future Reference" file drawer and a "Business Future Reference" file drawer. Each has its own set of hanging file folders. My Personal File Drawer has folders that say Apple, Bicycles, Camera, Delta, Edward Jones, Household, Instruction Manuals, Warranties, etc. All the necessary documents that I need to keep live in a file in this drawer. I name the file what the document is (Automobile Info) and file it alphabetically. So if my husband is looking for anything, it will be in

our Personal Reference Drawer filed alphabetically. The same goes for my Business Reference File Drawer. There are files for clients, marketing, social media, website, and then sub-folders for topics I collect information on such as clutter, self-defeating behaviors, technology, etc. The easiest way to name a file is to call the file what you would call the document category. The first name that comes to mind is usually what you would look for, so try calling it that. This doesn't need to be difficult, it needs to be simple and make sense to you.

So there you have it—the five steps you have for processing everything that comes into your life. When you complete this process of setting up your Command Central and touching everything to determine where it goes, you will end up with:

1. Only what you need, want or love remaining because you've tossed the rest.

2. Items that you either 1) will delegate and are now tucked in your Command Central on action cards to be done when you are back at your desk working, or 2) already delegated to others and are in a follow up system for tracking them. (Remember to take an "action card," write the task you delegated and place it in your system on the day before it's due to remind yourself that you are expecting it the next day. See the section on Action Cards on page 29.)

3. A bunch of "to do's" that either took two minutes or less to respond to, so you did—and they are no longer on your plate—or that are in your Command Central waiting to be done when you are back at your

desk working.

4. All your further action items that you have put in your daily or monthly files so that when the time comes, you will be reminded to do them.

5. A home for all non-action future reference items for you to access when you want to—or how about this, someone else can access because you now have an easy A-Z Future Reference File that even your colleagues and/or spouse can use.

Once you take the time to get yourself "up to date"—meaning you have tackled the piles everywhere and there is nothing else to process from your past build-up—all you have to do is process it day by day. And when you get in the habit of making quick decisions with everything, probably in about twenty-one days, you will be amazed at not only how good you get at it, but how freeing it feels to touch it, move it, and forget about it.

Now we're really talking turning your head off when you turn the lights off at night! Congratulations! You've earned it!

Prioritizing Made Easy

Now that you have essentially taken your "to do's" and put them in your system, all you have to do is prioritize your day, and if you really want to, you can get rid of your to-do list! Here's why I hate to-do lists. You have this long laundry list (on what I refer to as an *illegal* pad—I hate those things but that's for another discussion!) of all the things you have to do in your life. Some are personal, some are professional, but it's all-inclusive. Some need to be done this week, some need to be done next month. But so that you don't forget about them, they remain on your list. Then as you complete something, you cross it out. Now you can hardly distinguish the remaining outstanding "to do's" from the one's you've crossed out—so you flip the page and start another list. So the list never ends, and you never stop writing one. Ugh—what a mess of a system! All a list does is remind you of what you have to do, but it doesn't indicate when you have to do it. Sure, I have a ton of stuff to do but why would I want to carry around a list to stress me out about how much I have to do?

This is where those **3x5 "Action" Cards** come into play. Instead of putting all your to-do's on a list, put them on cards, one item per card. This way, you can then take that card and place it in the day or month in your Command Central for when you plan on doing it. Drop it in your Command Central and forget about it! You'll get to that day when it arrives and your to-do will be waiting for you.

Wendy's Juicy Tidbit #3

I have 3x5 cards with my logo and company information. I carry them with me when I go to a meeting. When someone in the meeting asks me to do something for them, (get them an email address or phone number, put together a proposal, etc.) I pull out a card and write the to-do on the card and when I get back to my office, I pop the card in my CC. I also give people information they may need from me on a card as well—it's another way of marketing your name and business out there in front of the world. People always ask me about my cards which means they take notice!

***The reason why I hate "illegal" pads so much is they quickly and frequently turn into BLACK HOLES for people. They take the pad to a meeting, take notes in the meeting, write to-do's in the margin of the notes page, then end the page and flip the page over and continue. The problem here is that they seldom flip those pages back to capture those to-do's and before you know it, they have dozens of flipped pages with who knows how many To Do's lurking in them. Keep notes on a pad, and your To Do's on cards—a much safer way to ensure remembering to do them.

With the Command Central, we have essentially turned your to-do list into a to-do system—a place where you only see/touch it when you need it next instead of seeing the same thing on your list for weeks unending. It's a challenge for those of you who treat your to-do list as if it's your Bible. I get it. But once you adopt this new habit and see how it feels to stop listing your day and start planning your day, you'll never want to make a list again. Now all you have to do is prioritize each day as it arrives and allow this system to offer the flexibility our lives ask of us. If you can't get to it today because something else became a bigger priority (and in most cases, plan for that to happen), move it to tomorrow and do it then. This system is not meant to be carved in stone. If you let it, it will be the flexible, adaptable, and simple solution to getting control of your workload and your life once and for all. Your to-do list will become a "ta-done" list. (Thank you Tim Phillips!)

Real Momentum Moment

Very shortly after we worked together, Tim Phillips of the American Cancer Society decided that this system could change the way he spent his day if he applied it and made it work for him. Now six years later, and most recently promoted to a top position, he institutes and values the tools he has gained to ensure he has control over his daily workload and his life.

Wendy's Juicy Tidbit #4

Look at your work week as a *FIVE DAY WINDOW*. Give yourself five days (Monday – Friday) to get all of that week's work done and try not to move your work into next week where your time is already committed. Command Central is made to be as flexible as our lives have to be. Give yourself some room to move something from Tuesday to Wednesday if need be. This takes the stress off having to stick to your original plan, but committing to Friday as your "drop dead date" for completing your work allows you to head into your weekend feeling like *YOU EARNED IT!*

Make Your Move Toward Momentum #3

Set up your Command Central while you're motivated and have the energy. Once that is complete, you can envision having nothing on your desk except what you are working on at any given moment. The only thing you should have on your desk every day is the daily folder for that day and the contents in it. Start working on the highest priority item and conclude with the lowest priority item. Be confident enough to know what needs to be done when and if you need to move projects/tasks around to accommodate your ever-changing life, do it with ease and assurance that tomorrow is another day—and it will get done.

Go to **www.wendyellin.com/bookdownloads** to order your Command Central tools.

Success does not make champions.
Challenges do.

Al Joyner

*I don't believe in email.
I'm an old-fashioned girl.
I prefer calling and hanging up.*

Sarah Jessica Parker

CHAPTER 4

Taming the Technology Tiger

I know…this is the topic you've all been holding out for, so let's not waste another minute. Email is commonly the #1 stressor among the people with whom I work when it comes to lost productivity. Like everything else that has real benefit, it can also be a real problem—it's in the way that you use it!

Here's the one really important thing that, if we'd all learned back in the 90's when email became a regular part of everyone's life, we wouldn't have nearly as many challenges with it as we do. Get ready—it's two words that can really change your life in relation to email if you get it, and you let it. Your email inbox was/ is only meant to be a **LOADING DOCK**. That's right…a LOADING DOCK! Now, unless I'm mistaken, nothing lives on a loading dock. A loading dock is a place for trains and trucks to temporarily drop off stuff that was in their compartments. But once they are unloaded there, they get moved to another place of residence. The dock is a space for loading and unloading—not a space for living or even hanging out for very long.

What do you do when your mail gets delivered to your house each day? I presume you go to the mailbox, take all the mail out, come into your house and if you are like me, you head straight to the kitchen trash can or recycle bin to sort through the junk. After tossing what I don't need (which is most of it), I put Marty's mail in his mail slot on the kitchen wall and take mine up to my office. I'm not saying we all do this, but I sure am hoping you do!

But picture this...you go down to your mailbox at the end of your driveway every afternoon and pull out just the mail that you want and leave the rest in the mailbox. Then tomorrow, you do the exact same thing—only take out what you need or want. Keep doing this for a few weeks and not only will you have a mailbox filled with junk (or clutter) but you will also frustrate your mailman who might eventually stop delivering to you, especially if he has nowhere to put it! Funny how when it comes to our physical mail that's delivered, most of us clean out the box every day. But when it comes to our email inbox, we let mail live in there until either our company warns us we are headed toward maximum capacity so that purging is your only option, or the amount of emails is haunting you because of the strong probability that something is about to fall through the cracks, if it hasn't already.

Now you officially have what is referred to as **ELECTRONIC CLUTTER**!

How do we tackle our electronic clutter to ensure it never gets to that level again? Well, we start with the same process we did for physical clutter and face every email in your inbox directly and promptly. We are going to process instead of put out fires, which is what most of you are doing; that is how all these un-attended emails wind up in your inbox. Then before you know it, you have electronic clutter. And now you're stressed out, defeated, overwhelmed, and headed to the break room vending machine or your kitchen freezer for ice cream. Process, people, **PROCESS**!

Starting now, we are going to take the same processing steps with everything that comes into our inbox. Yes, the same steps we take for paper we also take for email.

1. Let It Go
2. Let It Go to Someone Else
3. Do It Now
4. Further Action Folder (Command Central)
5. Future Reference Folder

But first, you need to set up places in your inbox for Future Reference and Further Action Folders.

Setting Up Future Reference Folders

Here you have some choices. You can either save an email in a folder that you create under your inbox so that you have easy access to anything while in your email program, or you can save an email to your hard drive. That's your call. But you can't have too many folders, because if they are not in folders, they will be in piles, which is exactly what 5,900 emails in your inbox is—one big electronic pile! Some of my folders under my inbox say clients, marketing, social media, Julie Rogers (Virtual Assistant), Kelly Powley (Speaking Agent), Growth Strategies (Social Media consultant), personal, self-development, technology, etc. And I have sub-folders under each of those. This way any time Stephen from Growth Strategies emails me something, it goes in his main folder if it's related to our agreement or general info, or it goes in a sub-folder such as LinkedIn, Twitter, Facebook, Website, Teleclasses, etc. When clients email me, the email goes in their specific client folder (if I want to keep the message). Remember, I'm only suggesting you keep what you need—in most cases there is a thread of emails from the same person so I only keep the most recent from that thread.

Setting Up Further Action Folders

Here are some options for the emails you need to TAKE FURTHER ACTION on:

1. Create a folder under the word Inbox. If you type an underscore before the folder title, the computer automatically puts this folder first. Otherwise it will appear alphabetically, and personally, I like these important folders that I use most frequently to be first. The first folder says **AWAITING MY RESPONSE (AMR)**. Everything that you have to do that takes longer than two minutes goes in that folder as it comes in. Then the next folder under that is **PENDING RESPONSE**. That is where you move an email to that refers to something you are waiting for from someone else. It is exactly like the Command Central **PR** file we created for our physical system.

Wendy's Juicy Tidbit #5

When I travel and I know I am not going to get to many of the things that come into my inbox while away, I will just pop that email into my AWAITING MY RESPONSE folder. It's great for getting all those future to-do's out of your inbox so it doesn't create mass clutter while you are traveling and so that you aren't stressed out by seeing all those to-do's" build up in your inbox while you are away.

2. Drag your action email over to your calendar. Your calendar feature will open and ask you what day you want to start and if you tell it July 31, when you save and close, it will appear on your calendar on July 31. Remember, I like to keep my to-do's off my calendar and only put my "to go's" on there, but you may want to have both. I support whatever works for you. There's never just one option for this stuff. As Tim Gunn (Project Runway) so cleverly says, "make it work" for you.

3. For those of you who use Microsoft Outlook and still have the 7 version, there is a feature in **TASKS** that works great for setting up a Command Central electronically. If you click on tasks, the default for viewing is what they call "simple list." But if you go down to the bottom of the viewing options and click on "task timeline," the **TASK** feature now acts as a 1-31 and January – December for you, just like the physical system. So if you have an email that requires your action, and you don't need to do it until next Thursday, August 16, drag that email to the word **TASK** in Outlook, the window opens and asks you when you want to start that task, give it a day, save and close, and that email will now show up on your Task Timeline under August 16. Then all you have to do is come in every day and click on **TASKS** and it will show you what's on your plate for that day. Two things to note about this feature are 1) when you drag an email from your inbox and save it in TASKS, it does not go out of the inbox so you still have to delete it, and 2) If it has an attachment that you need to work on, that won't transfer to TASKS so pop that original email into your **AWAITING MY RESPONSE** folder so that you have what you need to work from when the time comes.

4. Another option is to create folders under your inbox that each have a number (1-31) and a month (January-December) on them and drag emails into them

exactly the way you put paper in the physical system. Or you can create folders that say Week One, and have seven sub-folders under that, Week Two, with seven folders under that, etc. This is just a way to consolidate all those 1-31 folders.

5. The last option, which is the one I use the most, is to print out the email that you have to do and put it in your physical system to remind you that you have to start working on it, and also drag the email into the **AWAITING MY RESPONSE** folder. I like working a little with both systems and I'm always creating new and simple ways to make this system WORK FOR ME. Simple and flexible enough to accommodate your unique working situation is the key to the success of this system. And of course WORKING IT. No system out there will work unless you WORK IT.

There are so many different platforms, programs, and applications out there for communicating and staying organized: Lotus Notes, Outlook, Gmail, Evernote, I could go on and on. And stay tuned as there are plenty more on their way. What's most important is that whatever you choose to use, make sure it's easy enough for you to stay with it long enough to reap the benefits, or it will be a huge waste of time learning it and then ditching it shortly after.

Now with your Future Reference Folders and Further Action Folders in place, you are ready to sort through your Inbox and make one of five choices with every single email in there.

A quick note on sorting emails. The easiest way to sort through your inbox is to **SORT BY SENDER**. I have found, as most of my clients have, that sorting by Sender is the quickest way to get through all these emails that have built up in your inbox.

Which by the way, if I haven't said it loud enough...is just a **LOADING DOCK!** (Sorry, I just couldn't resist!) When sorting by Sender, the computer automatically alphabetizes your emails based on who they are from. Then you scroll down, one person/name at a time (and there could be 130 emails from a person/name) and if you know you don't need any of the emails from Sue Avery, delete them all at once. If you need some of them, make one of five choices and keep going. You keep deleting from the senders you no longer need to keep until you come to a bunch of emails from Harry Mood that you want to keep. You have forty-six of them, but since he's head of HR, you may want to refer to them at some point in the future. So do one of two things here: either create a reference folder to the left of your inbox that says "Harry Mood" or one that says "HR"—your call. If you think you'll want to put other HR related emails in there, then give Harry Mood his own folder. **YOU CAN'T HAVE TOO MANY FOLDERS.**

Quick Review of Five Steps to Take

1. **Let It Go.** How do you Let Go of an email? Delete it.

2. **Let It Go To Someone Else.** How do you Delegate an email? Forward it. A quick and easy way to track those that you delegate is to "blind copy" yourself on these and when they come back to you, drag them either to your tasks on the dates they are due, or put them in your Pending Response folder to track.

3. **Do It Now.** Remember, that's the "two minutes or less" rule, so as emails come into your inbox, if you can pop them out into someone else's "court" in two minutes or less, just do it. During this de-clutter process you can choose to either do all of these now or drag them to your AWAITING MY RESPONSE folder to do

when you have the time. It's all those quick emails that build up in your inbox that you don't process and then at the end of the day, you have thirty emails that could have taken two minutes or less to respond to and now it's an hour of your time. (I check my email at different times during my day for processing these exact ones—the ones I can get out of my inbox quickly. If you process even just a few "two minutes or less" emails throughout your day, you will have fewer emails in your inbox to deal with at the end of your day.)

4. **Future Reference Folder.** Simply click on an email or group of emails and drag them to the appropriate Future Reference Folder in your inbox or save to your hard drive.

5. **Further Action Folder.** Simply choose one of the options above, listed under Creating Further Action Folders, and move them out of your inbox!

Remember *Wendy's Juicy Tidbit #1*? Your life is like a VOLLEYBALL GAME and your goal is to get as many balls (in this case emails) out of your court (inbox) as possible and into someone else's. I'm a big subscriber to this for three reasons:

1) I like processing and getting things out of my court to be productive,

2) I like responding to people who may be waiting for something from me and if I can give it right back to them, I will, and

3) people generally treat me the same way I treat them so if I ask them for something that they can get right back to me, they do.

Basic Email Tips for Going Forward With Your New Electronic Command Central System

1. Remember that we are all in this together when it comes to the frustrating aspects of email.

2. Read your emails over before sending them—without the personal face-to-face communication, too many assumptions are derived from emails. Say what you want to say exactly like you would say it to them in person.

3. Get in and Get out – Say what you need to and not another word more. Your "wall of words" is a promise the reader will not read all the way to the end and a guarantee he/she will miss the most important point you are trying to get through.

4. Only reply to the people who need to receive it.

5. Use NRN – No Reply Necessary in your subject line if that's the case.

6. Use EOM – End of Message at the end of the subject line if that is the case.

7. Use NTN – No Thanks Necessary if that is the case.

8. Unsubscribe to at least five email lists per day. Deleting them will just make them go away for the day, but they'll be back in the morning! *(I unsubscribed to ten lists every day this week and am amazed at how few emails I am now receiving.)*

9. Schedule times during your day for processing. We all agree that, if all we did was sit in front of our computers all day and process email, we'd be plenty busy. But then when would our actual work get done? Focus on a project to

completion, then check your email and do some processing for thirty minutes, then back to work.

10. **REMEMBER THAT WE NEVER GET IT ALL DONE!** The minute we process all our emails and leave our desk to go to the bathroom, there are seventeen more emails in our inbox when we return. That's life—for all of us. Don't sweat it. Do as much as you can, put the rest in a place for when you need to see it next, and go enjoy your life.

Your life is waiting for you, and having an easy system for processing what comes in every day will allow you to approach it with positive energy, enthusiasm, and focus. Make THAT DAY'S WORK alone your goal for the day and nothing more. Feel great about what you have accomplished and know whatever didn't get done today will be waiting for you in YOUR NEW SYSTEM tomorrow.

Real Momentum Moment

This is a message from a client sent to his staff regarding Email Inbox Overage… "On our most recent bill from BlueWave was a charge for overage on our system backup. I have confirmed again that old Outlook messages do contribute to this overage charge. The chief offenders are large files with attachments. Remember that each time an email is sent, resent, forwarded, etc. that the attachment follows each time, and all of those are included in the overnight backup of the system. Please go through your Outlook folders and clean up everything you can. Start with the Large Mail folder and delete everything you can. The next step is to sort by sender and delete unnecessary messages. Thanks for your help to keep costs down." Looks like he "gets it"!

Make Your Move Toward Momentum #4

*Set up your Electronic Command Central System **NOW**! Follow the steps starting on page 43 to get yourself to a new "jumping off" place in your work, so that tomorrow when you come into your office and check your email inbox, all that is in there are the new emails that arrived overnight or that morning. And now that you have this new processing system, it will be a piece of cake to get through. Not only will you feel like you have more time to actually do your daily work, but you will also feel tremendous control over your workload. So now you are controlling it instead of it controlling you! Mission Accomplished!*

The Internet is the most important single development in the history of human communication since the invention of call waiting.

Dave Barry

*To do two things at once
is to do neither.*

Publius

CHAPTER 5

May I Please Have Your Undivided Attention?

There are a ton of books out there solely dedicated to the subject of multi-tasking. I've read quite a few of them, and I am not convinced by any argument that suggests multi-tasking is productive, pleasurable, or even possible! Trying to accomplish multiple tasks simultaneously doesn't increase your efficiency or productivity and does not make you feel good about your day at the end of it. That is my experience, and that sense of inefficiency and anxiety is confirmed by enough anecdotes and research that I'm convinced it's true for most others. Sometimes the attempt to combine distinct tasks is dangerous, like texting and driving. Sometimes it is ill-advised, like talking on the phone with one client and responding to the email of another. And sometimes it is innocuous, such as sizing your daughter's Girl Scout uniform while preparing the meat loaf. But it is rarely, and I mean rarely, a good idea to try.

Okay, there are certain functions you can perform at one time, such as walking on a treadmill while listening to headphones. I admit I frequently take my four-mile run/walk through my neighborhood while listening to a "self-development" workshop on my headphones. Not only am I burning calories and keeping my heart healthy, but I'm also actually gaining tremendous insight into either growing my business or growing myself. But research has shown that we don't use the same part of our brain for those two functions, so even if the exercise-walk-while-listening-to-headphones is an exception, too many of the things we try to save time by accomplishing at once require the same or overlapping functions of the brain, and we set ourselves up for problems.

Multi-tasking, or "switch-tasking" as Dave Crenshaw refers to it in his book *The Myths Of Multi-tasking*, is what this chapter and I are concerned about. And "switch-tasking," for me, is exactly how to describe what we all do all day long.

Picture this...you are on your computer cranking out a project that is due this afternoon by close of business. Your assistant drops something in your office inbox tray that has you curious, so you stop what you're doing to look it over. You see that there is a discrepancy in its content, so you pick up the phone to ask the author of this document about it. While on that call, an email pop-up alert tells you that you have a new email in your inbox regarding the appointment you have tomorrow morning at ten o'clock—they are looking for confirmation that you will be attending. So you put the call on hold for a minute to respond to that email—and at the same time someone IM's or PINGS you because they have an employee issue with someone on your team and want to get your input. HELP!

Now it's twenty-five minutes later, you've taken your thoughts and direction off of the computer project that is due at close of business, and with all the other distractions that you are allowing to absorb your attention—you are totally off course and unable to clearly and successfully attend to ANY OF THE TASKS IN FRONT OF YOU.

This is when I ask, "Does anything ever get your undivided attention?" In an instant, all these "To-Do's" are fighting for your attention that a mere twenty-five minutes ago did not even exist on your plate. And now you are trying to juggle all of them at the same time, hoping to accomplish each one professionally, accurately, and with the ATTENTION YOU KNOW THEY NEED AND DESERVE.

So, If your interruptions/distractions—call them what you want—aren't critical to that minute, here are my suggestions for how to handle these matters:

1) Stay with the project at hand. Do not stop your work to read the document that your assistant put in your office inbox tray until you choose to take a break. Curiosity has its time and place, but not when you have a deadline! Picking up the phone to inquire about this document that minute is moving you into dangerous distraction territory and you know it.

2) You can respond to that "confirmation" email when you take a break—it's a "two minutes or less" item to tell them you'll be there. They've waited until now to inquire; a few more minutes for your response won't kill them.

3) And as for the employee issue, if I'm the one waiting for your input, I would want your full attention on this, and if you tell me that you are in the middle of several things and that you will give me your full attention this afternoon (or even the next morning), I will be more inclined to wait if it means getting "all of you," focused and not distracted.

Dr. T. Jackson from Loughborough University, in his article entitled *Breaking Bad Habits: The Negative Effect of Email and Instant Messaging on the Workplace*, found that it takes 64 seconds to retrieve your train of thought after an interruption by email. That means if you check your inbox every five minutes, you waste 8.5 hours a week. My guess is that it takes just as long to retrieve your train of thought after an interruption by ANYTHING! So if possible stop letting it—whatever "it" is—interrupt you!

I so often hear the expression, "The only things we can be certain of are death and taxes." But in reality, we don't have to pay our taxes, right? That's a choice we get to make. The more realistic version of that would be…"The only thing that we can be certain of is death…and making choices." So in light of that, let's start getting better at the choices we make. Begin with the ones that seem small, like whether to answer that phone or start that conversation that you think may only take fifty seconds, but in actuality take fifty minutes.

The dictionary's definition of FOCUS is *"a point upon which attention, activity, etc, is directed or concentrated."* Really? Can you imagine in this day and age—with all our never-ending distractions—doing something like having a conversation with someone in your house and not also paying attention to the Olympics on the TV in the background, and gazing at the microwave to see how many seconds it has left until done, and trying to acknowledge your youngest child as he shares his daily art project with you ALL AT THE SAME TIME? Research shows that the average person loses focus six to ten times per minute! In fact, I'd venture a guess that six to ten times is somewhat of a low number. We exist in the bottomless pit of attention-grabbing opportunities 24/7/365. The only way to avoid it is to go to sleep…or choose to UNI-TASK for the sake of sanity, productivity, and a little self-control!

So here's what I propose for moving forward with as much focus and attention as you can possibly give ANYTHING YOU ARE DOING:

1. Commit to the process of completion. That's right, your goal is to set a short or long term goal for completing a project. If you come into your office in the morning and you know that you have a deadline of COB (Close of Business) that day, how many hours do you plan on devoting to that project today? Break it down into a morning session and an afternoon session if your day requires you to address other items in your "daily" folder. You get to make the choice as to how you spend your time every day. Choose it wisely and set yourself up for satisfaction and accomplishment, not frustration and failure.

2. Start communicating to your team/boss at work that you are trying to increase your daily efficiency and productivity and in doing so, you are asking for their support in seeing your work to completion before focusing on the next matter that needs your attention.

3. Build in "un-interrupted" hours in your day where everyone is focusing on their individual work and reserve the hour between 11-12 noon and 3-4 p.m. for "open interruption time." That means make yourself available for people who may need some answers from you to continue their productivity. Make sure there are at least TWO OPEN HOURS daily for staff to check in if necessary.

4. Place a **PLEASE DO NOT DISTURB** sign on your door asking that you not be disturbed, but also include a time in which you will be available to them and honor that time.

5. Remember that UNI-TASKING (working on one thing at a time) directly improves the quality of your work. Multi-tasking not only slows you down when it comes to productivity, it increases the chances of error that ultimately increases the time it takes for completion when you find yourself having to re-do your work.

6. Schedule appointments with yourself. Crazy as it sounds, if you block time out on your calendar every week to focus on your work, not only will you be more inclined to stay focused, but you will start to look forward to that time block where you can get substantial amounts of work completed. It's your time for whatever you want—even if it's for email processing, returning phone calls, or tying up loose ends.

7. If you work out of your home and have small children lurking around your office trying to get your attention, train them to interrupt you only at certain times of the day.

Real Momentum Moment

Terri, my client who worked out of her home office, had a red light bulb in her desk lamp. The door to her office was glass, which enabled her child to not only distract her, but also derail her from being productive on any given day. She told her child that when the red light was on, she was not to interrupt her. Only if it was off could she appear in front of the glass office door seeking attention. Brilliant idea and it worked.

Let's sum this up. Work against the habit to multi-task or "switch-task." Trying to do several things assures that none of them will get done as well as possible. Distinguish among the several matters vying for your attention. Prioritize them in order of importance, deadline or need to get them off your plate. Give your real focus to the one item that you have in front of you RIGHT NOW. Do great work, and move to the next with equal determination and focus. Honor the process, repeat the process—make the process YOUR RULE, NOT YOUR EXCEPTION!

Wendy's Juicy Tidbit #6

I refer to Fridays as CRAP DAY! That afternoon is reserved for all the little crap that I have to do in my work and in my life, such as entering contact information into my contact management program from business cards I collect all week. When I get them during the week, I toss them in my Friday file for that week, whatever that Friday's date is. Unless I'm traveling or it's a special client circumstance, I don't make any Friday afternoon appointments out of the office. I don't want to be stuck in Atlanta traffic on a Friday afternoon so it's a better use of my time to get all my "crap" done that day. And nothing feels better than going into my weekend feeling like I EARNED it!

Make Your Move Toward Momentum #5

Look at your calendar and see where you can create block times for doing your work. Maybe it means that every Monday and Wednesday between 8-11 a.m. you are going to work on what is in your Command Central for that day and stay focused for those three hours before stopping for interruptions. No answering phones, no checking emails, no surfing the Internet—just knocking those balls out of your court! Get your team on board with this notion of "un-interrupted" work hours every day and see how much more productive and efficient you will all be. And consider making Friday afternoons your "Crap Day" as well. You'll be glad you did!

Many people feel they must multi-task because everybody else is multi-tasking, but this is partly because they are all interrupting each other so much.

Marilyn Vos Savant

(One short comment on this quote… my girlfriends and I are constantly talking over each other, which frustrates my husband almost more than anything else I do! Actually not just me, ALL OF US WOMEN! He is continually amazed as to how we can have several conversations going at once, and somehow be attuned to each conversation while interrupting at every opportunity and ultimately not being bothered or fazed by it. And by the way, I'm not condoning this behavior, I'm just stating its irony!)

Better to be three hours too soon than one minute too late.

William Shakespeare

CHAPTER 6

Right on Time

All of the topics we have discussed thus far are central to the way I live my life with purpose, balance, and peace of mind. They are almost as fundamental as breathing, sleeping and eating are to my daily existence. But none of them resonates more with me on a personal or professional level than the subject of **BEING ON TIME**. And you'll notice that this is a subject rarely spoken about in daily conversation, unless you attend a specific session devoted to it, or read this chapter of my book!

It is rather amazing how many times in my life I have waited way past the scheduled appointment time for friends, clients, family members, and total strangers. I would venture to say that most of us spend an inordinate amount of time in our life just WAITING FOR SOMEONE. And honestly, it's not the waiting that stirs the emotional stuff up in me, but the fact that my time is not being respected by the one imposing the wait. I try to recognize that the people who are late are frequently kind and loving people who would never purposely disrespect me. However, their insensitivity when only considering their own agendas directly affects not only my time, but my attitude and opinion about their ability to honor their word. And in my opinion, being credible and honoring your word are the silent, yet essential, core values needed to maintain a relationship where truth, respect and integrity are the foundation.

Now, I have a role to play in this promptness dance, as we all do. This is when making choices comes back into play (as it does in virtually every interaction). We don't actually have to do nothing while we wait for those whose moral compass and time management skills don't match ours. And actually, we don't have to wait either! I use this time (when leaving isn't my choice) to pull out that **RIP & READ** file we spoke about in Chapter 4. Always presuming I will have a wait when going places, I just take my reading file with me so that at least I'm using that time to my advantage.

I recall several years ago when I was doing volunteer work for a non-profit that was forty-five minutes from my home. Their volunteer coordinator and I had set a time for a number of us to meet at 1 p.m. for lunch around the corner from their office, so I had a drive ahead of me. I arrived at 12:45 p.m., because after building in extra minutes for potential highway construction or midday traffic due to something unavoidable, I didn't want to take the chance of being late. It was 1:30 before my lunch dates arrived, with no acknowledgement whatsoever about their tardiness. I remember that evening sharing my frustration with Marty, about how I felt discounted by people I was donating my time to—it didn't feel right that they didn't honor the one thing I was giving them of myself...MY TIME! In the moment, it felt so personal, like I was the only one they treated that way, although I knew that wasn't the case at all. Marty reminded me, "Wendy, they didn't pick you out of all the people they know to behave to this way. This is not personal against you...my guess is that they don't even know they are 'doing anything wrong.'" And he was exactly right. Most people who are chronically late—which these people were on almost every occasion of our meeting—are not even remotely clued in that this is their behavior. It is the way they have been living their lives ALL OF THEIR LIVES. It's not meant to be a personal affront to any one person, it just is.

I ask you right now to grab a pen and paper and write down all the people in your life that are chronically late. I have no doubt that you will easily come up with five people, either in your personal or professional life, that fit that bill. Yes? (What is most amazing is not how many names you can come up with, but how fast those names will pop into your head!) Maybe you are even one of them? Think about that for a minute!

I have people I love in my life who are stubbornly resistant to growing a new understanding about the importance of this issue. Frequently, when Marty and I are dressing to entertain certain friends on a Saturday night, I find myself in the closet thinking and sharing under my breath, but loud enough for him to hear me, "Don't hurry, they're never here on time." And here's the REALITY ABOUT THIS...no matter what else is true about these people, they are labeled as 'late,' and it impacts my relationship with them. ***WE EARN OUR REPUTATION EITHER WAY!*** You will ultimately have a reputation of being an on-time person or a late person— and the difference is this: having the reputation of being a late person doesn't require much effort on your part. But being an on-time person not only TAKES EFFORT—IT TAKES TIME. YOUR TIME. AND IT'S WORTH THAT EFFORT AND THE INVESTMENT OF YOUR TIME!

My clients will often moan, "You mean I have to have more time just to be on time? I don't have enough time in my day as it is and you want me to have more?" And the answer is YES. Because in order to be on time, you have to build in time to get where you are going. Sounds simple in theory, but somewhat more difficult in reality. Especially if you are new to changing this habit. More on this in a minute.

Timeliness is an issue that always involves two parties, those who are late and those doing the waiting for those who are late. And for many, the question of respect never comes up. I think that this is the way they have always navigated through their days and are not even attuned to how it may affect others, because being timely is not a conversation we tend to have often, lightly or directly for the sake of courtesy or respect, much less reputation!

I remember when I was selling radio ads back in the early 90's. I had several clients who were in Buford, Georgia, which was at least forty-five minutes from either my home or the radio station. The common question for me was "Do I call the client to confirm my appointment with them and take the chance that they will cancel it if I do, or just drive out there and hope that they remember the appointment and are actually present?" My dilemma was honoring my word and risk wasting time, or not honoring my word and risk standing up my client,

In light of this very discussion, the following is a letter written to me by a client and a friend regarding what she is now experiencing since adapting a **BE ON TIME** attitude and new way of living. This followed our open and honest discussion about not what I wanted out of her being on time, but what she could potentially experience. I'm not sure I could put it into words better than she.

Real Momentum Moment

"I juggle a lot of balls in my day, I over commit, and most of the time I underperform in the context of being on time. Recently, Wendy pointed out to me that your reputation with respect to timeliness precedes you and often defines how others perceive you in far reaching ways. Her comments resonated and made me realize that I did not want to be known as a person who is never on time, who consequently is seen as someone who doesn't respect other people's time, who is frantically rushing from place to place, and I did not want to continue to be someone who begins each encounter apologizing for being late.

I made a decision to change and it has profoundly impacted how I move through my day and my relationships with others. It is an unexpected feeling of freedom and one that merits sharing. All it took was a few simple steps (with Wendy's guidance) and some self-awareness to do things differently.

First, I had a terrible habit of trying to tie up loose ends before leaving my home or office: I would make a few phone calls, shoot off a couple of emails, take out the trash, and tidy up. While those things may have been important to do, I always waited until the last minute to do them and they always took longer than I had planned.

Next, I realized that I had no concept of how long it took to get out of my house or office, then to my car, and then to the place I need to be. I never took into consideration things like traffic, events going on in the city which cause congestion on the road, or that I needed to build in time to familiarize myself with a place, route, or area I have never been to before. I have made the decision to think about these considerations and leave myself plenty of time to get where I am going.

Now, rather than aggressively driving to get to places on time or fill my headspace with what I was going to tell the person to justify my tardiness, I now enjoy being in the car. I listen to my favorite tunes and I have the appropriate headspace to prepare myself for my arrival at whatever meeting or appointment I am on my way to. Before, it would take me several minutes once I arrived to just decompress from the frantic and rushed experience of getting there. I couldn't really be fully present once I got to where I was going because I was still unraveling the unnecessary energy that was forced upon me because of my poor planning.

People have taken notice of the change, and while that feels good, it feels even better to know that it was possible to change and to take simple steps to being a more thoughtful and mindful person about how my time impacts me and others."

Wow! Not only did she get it, but it was no longer than a few days after our initial discussion when she shared this experience with me, which means it didn't take long to acknowledge, accept, and consciously correct the problem. And as she shared above, the positive implications it immediately had on her life, not only served as ongoing incentive, but also provided the good feeling she longed for that will ultimately change her reputation. I'd say that's a win/win...don't you think?

Here are some things you can do immediately that will not only enhance good feelings as you move through your day, they will ensure that you are no longer identified in the "late" category again. Yes, there will always be circumstances you cannot avoid. But if you replace your reputation with "on time" instead of "late," not only will you not feel as bad when the unavoidable circumstance is upon you, but those waiting for you will look at it, and you, differently.

1. Decide that you are going to be "ON TIME." That means whatever it takes, you are in. NOT half in. FULLY 100% in. Start seeing yourself on time everywhere you go. Even see yourself early with time to read one article before the other party arrives. Or use that time to return a call or just enjoy the few extra minutes in your day to do nothing. What a concept!

2. If you find yourself the one on the "waiting" side, consider having a conversation with those in your life whose tardiness impedes your relationship by disallowing the authentic experience you would like. An open, honest dialog of what an authentic relationship would look like to you may not only help you attain that, but your enlightening them may be a far-reaching exercise where many win.

Wendy's Juicy Tidbit #7

This is where being on time TAKES TIME! If you have an appointment on your calendar for 10 a.m., 2 p.m. and 4 p.m., you no longer have just three appointments. You now have six appointments—you have a 9:30 a.m. appointment to get out of wherever you are to get to that 10 a.m. appointment ON TIME. You have a 1:30 p.m. appointment to get to your 2 p.m. appointment ON TIME and a 3:30 p.m. appointment to get to your 4 p.m. appointment ON TIME. That's right, six appointments. I put a TT next to the time on my calendar for Travel Time. If you don't schedule the travel time necessary to get to a place on time, it will most likely not happen. That means leaving your office or home at 9:30 a.m. without answering the ringing phone as you exit, without emptying the trash can on your way out, and without checking your email one last time before charging for the door.

Granted, we can all find a million things that need to be done in our lives if we look—just don't look and do when you have somewhere to be. Make that the focus of your attention and when you do, here is some of what you will experience:

1. You will arrive on time and nothing feels better than this, especially if it is new to you!

2. You will not be stressed out from the pace you were keeping just to get there.

3. You will be more mentally prepared for your meeting, which will promote a more productive outcome.

4. You will not be frazzled, but instead emotionally and physically available for the remainder of your day. That means even getting to your next appointments on time as well—you're right on schedule and moving with *Momentum!*

5. You will feel great about yourself and what you have accomplished by caring, planning, and following through on your decision to make it happen and be on time.

6. Not only will this way of life be "habit" changing, it will be a "game" changer in the way you live your life in relation to your self-respect, as well as your respect for others.

Make Your Move Toward Momentum #6

Look at your calendar going forward. Wherever there is an appointment with a designated start time, put a TT on your calendar thirty minutes before the meeting starts. Do that for every scheduled appointment and make a point to honor that EVERY TIME. Let the last minute things you tend to do while running out the door wait until you return. Nothing will happen if they don't get done that minute, I promise. And I also promise that the benefits you'll derive from being on time will be well worth your effort and the extra time it takes to make it happen. Here's to your success...and potentially new reputation!

A note about my husband: *When I met Marty, he was habitually late. He always assumed he could get there, no matter where "there" was, faster than real life would allow. He was always willing to be forgiven, and is charming enough that people most often readily forgave him. But based on a little nudge from his bride, he saw the issue from a respect perspective and changed his habit quickly, and he is now on time much more often than not. And he now exercises another choice: he tells those with whom he has plans that he expects meetings, etc. to begin promptly. Yes, he believes it is within his right to expect promptness, but more importantly he believes it is essential to share with others how critical it is to him to honor plans that have been agreed to. So now, instead of being habitually late, he is happily making converts to the concept of timeliness.*

*I've been on a calendar,
but I've never been on time.*

Marilyn Monroe

Time is what we want most,
but what we use worst.

William Penn

CHAPTER 7

Get Realistic About Productivity

In Chapter 6, we spoke about time in relation to punctuality. Here I speak of time in relation to how we use those precious twenty-four hours we are given every day. And the sooner we become realistic about how we spend our time, the easier it will be to accept those hours as enough, because let's face it...we are never getting any more than those daily twenty-four hours.

By now, it should be clear from the previous chapters that there are countless items that require the use of your time. Between processing both mail and email, returning phone calls, completing projects, preparing, eating and cleaning up from meals, tending to children, commuting to and from work, building in time to be on time and a whole host of other things I haven't yet mentioned—it would seem easy to draw the conclusion that twenty-four hours is not nearly enough time to get our life done.

But here is where we get into real trouble...we live as if we have thirty-four hours in our day, not twenty-four! We schedule ourselves as if we have more time than we actually do. We see a calendar with time slots on it and nothing next to them, so we fill them up. We book ourselves solid from 8 a.m. to 8 p.m., and then we wonder why we didn't get it all done. Not only do we wonder about it, we are frustrated and disappointed in ourselves (or others), because we are left with incomplete or unfinished business.

No kidding! The reality of this is that all of what you scheduled to get done for that day wasn't going to get done to start with. It would have been impossible! So we start out of the gate every morning, setting ourselves up for failure. I don't think that was the way God meant for us to spend our days—over-committing, under-delivering, and left with a feeling of disappointment and defeat. So why don't we just start living as if we have twenty-four hours, and get realistic with how we use them as if our happiness depended on it? Oh, and by the way, it actually does!

I have spent many years working with people who are burned out, unhealthy, unmotivated, disillusioned and just plain tired of the pace with which they have been trying to keep up, as they struggle to be the best attorney, doctor, manager, assistant, spouse, student, whatever they can be. In reality, if they would slow down long enough to reevaluate how they use their time, they would find themselves so much closer to a place of genuine satisfaction and even passion than they are now by trying to "do it all" all the time.

Real Momentum Moment

After I left radio advertising sales, I ventured back into the radio world, excited to help increase efficiency and productivity in the lives of the sales people. I was in the offices of a local Atlanta radio station when the General Manager asked me "How many appointments do you think our sales people should be making per day?"

My answer was easy, "Let's go over to your window and look out there to see what is happening on GA 400?"

As it happened, his office overlooked one of the main arteries in Atlanta. And luckily for my desire to make a point, the traffic was almost at a stand-still in the middle of the day. "Do you see what is going on out there?" was my response.

You see, if you have ever been in sales, you are familiar with the phrase "it's a numbers game." How many face-to-face appointments do you need to have to increase your sales? When I was selling radio, it was all about the number of people you saw face-to-face on a daily basis. So I wanted to confirm that those "rules" still applied eleven years later. And I was not surprised to find (and I actually very much support the notion) that sales is still ultimately about relationships and those need to be started and nurtured in person.

That being said, there are two ways to actually handle what my client was asking about. The first is (and I'm not a big proponent) to tell your manager what they want to hear. If they want you to make five face-to-face sales calls per day, totaling twenty-five per week, then tell them that is what you will do. But being the realistic person I consider myself to be in most situations, I would rather set myself up for success by only committing to three per day. That would look like one in the morning, before noon, one in the afternoon before end of day, and if you can have a meeting over lunch, then add a third. Lunch hour meetings don't necessarily require the eating of lunch, but require a prospect/client being willing to meet over the lunch hour. This way you are building in time not only to prepare properly for each meeting, you are also building in enough time to get there on time, be productive while there, and then approach the rest of your appointments with the same prepared energy and attitude it takes to be successful at what you do.

I think my suggestion and reasoning resonated enough with him to agree that being prepared, on time and effective for each sales call trumped telling him what he may have wanted to hear.

If getting reasonable and realistic about how much you can get done in a twenty-four hour period is something you care to embrace, you may want to consider some options:

1. Stop pretending. Stop assuming that the only way you can be satisfied, gainfully employed, or successful is to do more and more and more. Sometimes, it is much more important to do less very well than to do even more less well.

2. Build in BLOCK TIMES (as mentioned in Chapter 6) as appointments with yourself to get your project work done. Or use that time for returning phone calls, processing email, or for whatever loose ends need tying up.

3. Make sure to include TT (Travel Time) on your calendar for ensuring you get to your appointments on time. I don't know where you live, but if the city you navigate every day is anything like Atlanta, you should not plan to get anywhere in under twenty minutes. Remember, just when you think that you can get there with minutes to spare, the neighborhood water main is under repair and your one lane of traffic each way takes all the wind out of your sails!

4. Keep a Daily Time Tracker for a week to see where you are using your time. That means really pay attention and write down how you are using each minute/hour. If you are in a profession that bills by the hour and your income depends on it, you are no stranger to the world of time tracking. But spending a week really clued into how you spend your day will not only be a revealing exercise, but one also that might steer

you in a new direction when it comes to how you plan your day and allot your time. Once you have tracked it, there should be obvious places where you can adjust your thinking and your doing to get to the end of your day experiencing satisfaction, accomplishment, and confidence.

5. Do what you can, do it the best that you know how, and leave what is left for tomorrow.

Make Your Move Toward Momentum #7

Starting tomorrow morning, and for an entire week, write down how you use your time from the minute you awaken until the minute you go to sleep. Include the personal time you spend as well as the work time to give you an accurate accounting of what your day looks like and where you can adjust it to accommodate your preferred lifestyle. No time for exercise? Maybe get up an hour earlier every morning. Spending too much time in your car every day? Consider revising your commuting schedule to maximize productivity in your workday. Make a list of the things you want your life to be filled with and find a way to carve the time out for exactly that!

Time is really the only capital that any human being has, and the only thing he can't afford to lose.

Thomas Edison

*Don't let the perfect
get in the way of the good.*

Arne Duncan

CHAPTER 8

Quit Sabotaging Yourself!

There are a few self-defeating behaviors that, despite any attempts we make to rid ourselves of them, somehow seem to creep back into our being. I won't spend too much time on any of these for two reasons. One is that there is so much research devoted to these subjects that reading a book solely dedicated to each would offer you far greater insight than I offer here. And second, I'm sticking with my theory that what we focus on expands. And since not one of these issues is one I'm interested in you keeping around, I'll touch lightly for the sake of reminding you to address them directly and to get them promptly behind you. Give their history of keeping you ineffective/unproductive as little attention as you can. Be in charge of your behaviors; when you stop allowing them to dictate your responses to possible roadblocks, you will no longer need to give them attention.

PROCRASTINATING: Let's start with this one since EVERYONE ALWAYS LEAVES IT FOR LAST! It's common to all, a universal behavior that ultimately does not serve you well—ever. There are at least a handful of reasons why we procrastinate even knowing and admitting we shouldn't; all of them easy to use as an excuse, yet none of them valid. And the interesting thing about procrastinating is that most of the time, the task we are putting off is not nearly as bad as we think.

Here's the key...it's the STARTING of the task that we can't seem to get to, not the completion of the task. And you must begin to be able to conclude, hence the trouble.

The easiest solution for no longer putting things off is to commit to the starting of a project first. Put a date/time on your calendar when nothing else can get in the way of your starting and, if necessary, only bite off the project bits at a time. Remember, you just need to start it, or start the next piece, not necessarily finish it then.

Real Momentum Moment

I recall when working in radio sales and it came time to come up with a sales budget for the upcoming year—it was clearly the one singular thing I disliked most in that job. So after many years of putting it off until the day before it was due and staying up nearly all night to complete it, I decided to split my client list into quarters and only tackle one quarter per night until, after four nights, the budget was complete. I tackled the first piece to the best of my ability, then the next piece the next night and so on, and after parceling it out like I finally did, the project wasn't anywhere near the obstacle it initially appeared to be. Now don't get me wrong, I didn't all of a sudden love this project, but it no longer had a hold on me like it had in the past. It was an inevitable part of my job that, once I had a plan, worked well enough to repeat over the years.

I am also big on rewards. That's right, arrange a reward for yourself, any kind of reward, for getting to something that appeared painful at the onset but that you started anyway. Give yourself a pat on the back and an hour to take your puppy to the park if that is what you enjoy. Head to Starbucks for that afte   uccino. Whatever it is, make it worth the effort to get int   ting off—MAKE A DENT and it will make a

PERFECTIONISM: What a difficult concept t   e goal for most projects. What an impossib   r. And yet...what a worthy goal to strive fc

The trick here is to strive for excellence,   st, to accept your humanity. By that I mec   est result you can produce even if it is not

I'm a huge subscriber to the opening qu   g...

> *"Don't let the PERFECT g*

For me, if it represents the most that   p for success and fully focusing on the pro   vious chapters), my best is good enough   new

PERFECT! This way, GREAT will not only be attainable (unlike PERFECT), but it's a much better use of my time and energy than fretting about not being PERFECT. Most of my days are filled with positive, engaging, productive experiences that I conclude are great. And that's just good enough for me!

As I spend more time in a business turned on its side by the recent recession, I see an increasing number of people who, quite honestly, just don't have time for perfection. They have been asked to do more with less, and they are just trying to keep afloat and get control of their lives the best they know how. They fret that their work product will necessarily diminish because the volume of requests for their time and talent is increasing, and their resources are diminishing. What a perfect time to remember two things:

1) Organize the many tasks coming at you the best you can. Take to heart the advice of the previous chapters about how to prioritize, how to delegate, how to respond to interruptions etc. and prepare yourself as well as possible to do great work.

2) Great work is to be celebrated. This is NOT to say you or those you work with should lower your sights or accept a work product that is beneath you or that is not all that you can achieve. But it is a strong message that sometimes you must take pride and pleasure in a product that is less than the perfect you tried to reach. One more thought—people who strive only for perfection can never be totally satisfied with anything less, and the ongoing battle reality creates only sets them up for failure on some level.

WORKAHOLISM: The message here is an obvious one, but one that seems hard to embrace—if you give everything to any one facet of your life, the rest of your life will wither from inattention.

The siren song of "stay longer and do more" at the job is impossible for most of us to ignore. But if you are worn down, if you have tried to accomplish too many things and never take a break or have the chance to do discrete pieces of your work as well as possible—if you are just tapped out—you risk having nothing to give to your job, your family, yourself. It is becoming ever so clear that when your mental and physical health is at risk from not being able to control your drive to work, you are literally left with nothing to actually work with. And eventually that is what most workaholics are faced with. Worn out, energy-depleted, too depressed to be effective in their work, and much less productive. Suffice it to say that there is so much more to life than work, no matter what you do.

I feel incredibly blessed to do something in this world that I am completely, 100% passionate about—to the point where it doesn't feel like work and I could do it all day long. But even having said that, we (including myself) all need a break in the action—any action. Change and some re-charging time are essential to maintaining a clear, focused path from which to create whatever your passion is in this world.

Make Your Move Toward Momentum #8

Start to look at where some of these self-defeating behaviors stick out in your life. Are you a major procrastinator? If so, make a list of the tasks on which you are procrastinating. Put each one on a 3x5 Action Card and then place that card in your Command Central on the day you plan to start that item. That's a great first step, and you have to start somewhere!

Is the desire for Perfect getting in the way of your Good, or Great? If so, spend some time visualizing what outcome you could be really satisfied with and make that your end goal. Don't call it anything, just see it in its final state. That might make the journey to get there more enjoyable and attainable.

For those of you who find yourselves leaning toward workaholic behavior, start building in "personal break" time to actually stop what you are working on and do something that requires a different part of your brain function. Take a walk, play with the dog, run an errand, anything to change things up for you and break the "work" cycle you are on and can't seem to get off. Make sure to build in breaks throughout the day to avoid the burnout, energy depletion, and increased stress you may commonly experience.

In short...Get To It, Let Great Be Good Enough, and remember that Too Much of Any One Thing isn't always the answer!

Nothing is so fatiguing as the eternal hanging on of an uncompleted task.

William James

Good habits are worth being fanatical about.

John Irving

CHAPTER 9

Where Do You Go from Here?

Here is the truth about my insights. They are my insights. This is my perspective, my experience and my reality. They are what work for me to experience the momentum I want for my life. And while that doesn't mean they will absolutely work in the same exact way for you, many of them just might. You have options that will allow you to move away from what is not working toward what will. If you are tired of swimming upstream in your life, try some of these ideas on for size. See how they fit on you and into your life. Practice them for a while; experience the difference that going with this flow makes. Pay close attention, and start to recognize how living with new habits makes you feel. Because the big question that all of this boils down to is: How does it make you feel?

Feelings that do not promote excitement, satisfaction, growth or happiness, I would urge you to do something different about so that the outcome—and the feeling derived from the outcome—yield greater reward. (Your greater reward, not mine.) Remember, it's your reason, your "why?"; your vision of what you want the new picture of your life to look like that starts you on this road of change to begin with and keeps you on it indefinitely.

I am not exactly where I want to be, although I am working hard to move toward that goal. And what my goal looks like may look totally different than yours. But how I go about my daily life not only continues to make me happy, but also ensures my alignment with who I really am and allows me to be more conscious of my time and my experiences every single day. By being purposeful and aware, and by working hard, I get more out of every minute and look forward to what else is waiting in my future.

I hope this information awakens and empowers you enough to shift your thinking in the direction of action. We are all on this great adventure called life, where each of us is our own producer, director, and the star! We get to decide and create what we envision for ourselves and seek change as we experience moments, expand our thinking and learn new ways of doing things. Take responsibility for where you are in your current circumstances. Whatever you choose to do from this moment forward, be intentional. Have your outcome in mind and be remarkable in your steadfastness to reach it.

Joy is within reach for each of us. Your changes are your destiny. Choose your direction, commit to the behavior, and experience what consistent effort, dedication and passion have in store for you. Then please come share your transformation with me—I can't wait to hear about it!

Here's to your success, and thank you for allowing me to have with you this open and candid conversation about choices.

Go to **www.wendyellin.com/bookdownloads** to order your Command Central tools.

People will not change unless something in them changes.

Unknown

*Nothing stands between you
and permanent happiness.*

Guy Finley

Wendy's Juicy Tidbits

Wendy's Juicy Tidbit #1

Look at your business life like one big VOLLEYBALL GAME – your goal is to get as many balls out of your court and into someone else's every day, whether they come in by mail, email, text, voicemail, etc. It doesn't mean that they won't come back to you, but at least you are moving them out of "your court," which means productivity is happening.

Wendy's Juicy Tidbit #2

Distinguish between "where you go" and "what you do" on a daily basis. That means don't have your "to go's" and your "to do's" in the same place. My "to go's" go on my calendar because they relate to a specific time (i.e., lunch appointment, client meeting, conference call, doctor appointment, etc.) My "to do's" go in my Command Central in the day that I want to get started on a certain project, or when it is due, depending on how long it takes to complete. I put my appointments on my calendar and then anything, like directions to that appointment, go in my CC on the day of the appointment.

Wendy's Juicy Tidbit #3

I have 3x5 cards with my logo and company information. I carry them with me when I go to a meeting. When someone in the meeting asks me to do something for them, (get them an email address or phone number, put together a proposal, etc.) I pull out a card and write the to-do on the card and when I get back to my office, I pop the card in my CC. I also give people information they may need from me on a card as well—it's another way of marketing your name and business out there in front of the world. People always ask me about my cards which means they take notice!

Wendy's Juicy Tidbit #4

Look at your work week as a FIVE DAY WINDOW. Give yourself five days (Monday – Friday) to get all of that week's work done and try not to move your work into next week where your time is already committed. Command Central is made to be as flexible as our lives have to be. Give yourself some room to move something from Tuesday to Wednesday if need be. This takes the stress off having to stick to your original plan, but committing to Friday as your "drop dead date" for completing your work allows you to head into your weekend feeling like YOU EARNED IT!

Wendy's Juicy Tidbit #5

When I travel and I know I am not going to get to many of the things that come into my inbox while away, I will just pop that email into my AWAITING MY RESPONSE folder. It's great for getting all those future to-do's out of your inbox so it doesn't create mass clutter while you are traveling and so that you aren't stressed out by seeing all those to-do's" build up in your inbox while you are away.

Wendy's Juicy Tidbit #6

I refer to Fridays as CRAP DAY! That afternoon is reserved for all the little crap that I have to do in my work and in my life, such as entering contact information into my contact management program from business cards I collect all week. When I get them during the week, I toss them in my Friday file for that week, whatever that Friday's date is. Unless I'm traveling or it's a special client circumstance, I don't make any Friday afternoon appointments out of the office. I don't want to be stuck in Atlanta traffic on a Friday afternoon so it's a better use of my time to get all my "crap" done that day. And nothing feels better than going into my weekend feeling like I EARNED it!

Wendy's Juicy Tidbit #7

This is where being on time TAKES TIME! If you have an appointment on your calendar for 10 a.m., 2 p.m. and 4 p.m., you no longer have just three appointments. You now have six appointments—you have a 9:30 a.m. appointment to get out of wherever you are to get to that 10 a.m. appointment ON TIME. You have a 1:30 p.m. appointment to get to your 2 p.m. appointment ON TIME and a 3:30 p.m. appointment to get to your 4 p.m. appointment ON TIME. That's right, six appointments. I put a TT next to the time on my calendar for Travel Time. If you don't schedule the travel time necessary to get to a place on time, it will most likely not happen. That means leaving your office or home at 9:30 a.m. without answering the ringing phone as you exit, without emptying the trash can on your way out, and without checking your email one last time before charging for the door.

*An unexamined life
is not worth living.*

Socrates

Make Your Move
Toward *Momentum*

Make Your Move Toward *Momentum* Intro

Spend a few minutes writing down your reasons for changing the way you live. What would doing things differently look like? What's not working that you think having a new system for living your life would fix? What's in it for you? Why change your daily habits around how your environment functions?

*It's the power of the **Why?** that directly affects the outcome of the challenge! Make sure your reason or reasons hold so much value for you that there is no turning back until it's your new reality.*

Make Your Move Toward *Momentum* #1

Every morning before you start your day, sit quietly for a few minutes and envision what that day will look like. Literally see yourself navigating through your day, moving from place to place, getting to your appointments on time (or a little early), connecting positively with people in person or on the phone, getting your work done, and arriving back home at the end of the day with a huge sense of accomplishment and satisfaction. You have a much better chance of what you envision actually happening if you do this rather than winging it and hoping it turns out this way. Remember, getting it in your HEAD first starts the ball rolling in that direction.

Make Your Move Toward *Momentum #2*

*Put a date on the calendar **RIGHT NOW** for the de-cluttering session and follow the four steps on page 12. Invite someone to join you who has your best interest at heart. Turn up the tunes and make this fun—you will be amazed at how enjoyable the purging process is once you get started. You'll let go of things you never thought you could part with—and before you know it, you'll feel lighter on your feet and the things that really matter will appear more clear and focused. Here's to your success!*

Make Your Move Toward *Momentum #3*

Set up your Command Central while you're motivated and have the energy. Once that is complete, you can envision having nothing on your desk except what you are working on at any given moment. The only thing you should have on your desk every day is the daily folder for that day and the contents in it. Start working on the highest priority item and conclude with the lowest priority item. Be confident enough to know what needs to be done when and if you need to move projects/tasks around to accommodate your ever-changing life, do it with ease and assurance that tomorrow is another day—and it will get done.

Make Your Move Toward *Momentum #4*

*Set up your Electronic Command Central System **NOW**! Follow the steps on page 41 to get yourself to a new "jumping off" place in your work, so that tomorrow* *when you come into your office and check your email inbox, all that is in there are the new emails that arrived overnight or that morning. And now that you have this new processing system, it will be a piece of cake to get through. Not only will you feel like you have more time to actually do your daily work, but you will also feel tremendous control over your workload. So now you are controlling it instead of it controlling you! Mission Accomplished!*

Make Your Move Toward *Momentum* #5

Look at your calendar and see where you can create block times for doing your work. Maybe it means that every Monday and Wednesday between 8-11 a.m. you are going to work on what is in your Command Central for that day and stay focused for those three hours before stopping for interruptions. No answering phones, no checking emails, no surfing the Internet—just knocking those balls out of your court! Get your team on board with this notion of "un-interrupted" work hours every day and see how much more productive and efficient you will all be. And consider making Friday afternoons your "Crap Day" as well. You'll be glad you did!

Make Your Move Toward *Momentum* #6

Look at your calendar going forward. Wherever there is an appointment with a designated start time, put a TT on your calendar thirty minutes before the meeting starts. Do that for every scheduled appointment and make a point to honor that EVERY TIME. Let the last minute things you tend to do while running out the door wait until you return. Nothing will happen if they don't get done that minute, I promise. And I also promise that the benefits you'll derive from being on time will be well worth your effort and the extra time it takes to make it happen. Here's to your success...and potentially new reputation!

Make Your Move Toward *Momentum* #7

Starting tomorrow morning, and for an entire week, write down how you use your time from the minute you awaken until the minute you go to sleep. Include the personal time you spend as well as the work time to give you an accurate accounting of what your day looks like and where you can adjust it to accommodate your preferred lifestyle. No time for exercise? Maybe get up an hour earlier every morning. Spending too much time in your car every day? Consider revising your commuting schedule to maximize productivity in your workday. Make a list of the things you want your life to be filled with and find a way to carve the time out for exactly that!

Make Your Move Toward *Momentum* #8

Start to look at where some of these self-defeating behaviors stick out in your life. Are you a major procrastinator? If so, make a list of the tasks on which you are procrastinating. Put each one on a 3x5 Action Card and then place that card in your Command Central on the day you plan to start that item. That's a great first step, and you have to start somewhere!

Is the desire for Perfect getting in the way of your Good, or Great? If so, spend some time visualizing what outcome you could be really satisfied with and make that your end goal. Don't call it anything, just see it in its final state. That might make the journey to get there more enjoyable and attainable.

For those of you who find yourselves leaning toward workaholic behavior, start building in "personal break" time to actually stop what you are working on and do something that requires a different part of your brain function. Take a walk, play with the dog, run an errand, anything to change things up for you and break the "work" cycle you are on and can't seem to get off. Make sure to build in breaks throughout the day to avoid the burnout, energy depletion, and increased stress you may commonly experience.

In short...Get To It, Let Great Be Good Enough, and remember that Too Much of Any One Thing isn't always the answer!

*You must learn to stop thinking in terms of beginnings and endings, successes and failures, and begin to treat life as a **learning** experience instead of a **proving** one.*

Guy Finley

About Wendy

As Atlanta based Workplace Productivity Strategist, Wendy Ellin is dedicated to helping people 'love what you do and *LOVE THE WAY YOU DO IT*' through a variety of organizational systems, tools and techniques.

Wendy came to the organizing industry with over twenty years of corporate business, sales and entrepreneurial experience. Her roles in radio sales, radio sales management and executive administration give her a broad perspective on what it takes to be organized and successful in business.

She developed The *Momentum* Method to meet the needs of businesses, organizations and individuals who can benefit from having foolproof systems for running their professional and personal lives.

The *Momentum* Method includes processes for making quick, simple decisions that yield sustainable results in every aspect of your life. It's these simple techniques that help jumpstart *momentum* in everything you do.

Wendy's approach to training is engaging, interactive, and with a "let's make a difference in your life" attitude. She is 100% passionate about helping clients develop solutions to a wide variety of problems related to lack of organization. Her goal is not to change who you are, but to change the way you address your challenges for the sole purpose of having *momentum* in your life.

Wendy has two grown step-daughters, Blair and Leah. She and her husband Marty Ellin, an attorney, live in Atlanta with their golden doodle, Ruby.

What is The *Momentum* Method?

The founding principle of The *Momentum* Method is the belief that success breeds success. Having *momentum* in your life is fundamental to being happy. It means you have less stress, more free time, and peace of mind. It eliminates chaos and disorganization and can boost your self-confidence as well as your outlook on life.

And just like disorganization doesn't happen overnight, it takes time to truly change the way you live and work. The *Momentum* Method teaches you to take on one new habit or change at a time, internalize it and see how it delivers a positive outcome. Then you make the next change. And the next one. And pretty soon, you're living differently, benefiting from the results, and that's when you see how easy it is to not only love what you do, but to also *LOVE THE WAY YOU DO IT.*

Acknowledgements

This book could not have happened had it not been for those whose ongoing support and encouragement kept me on schedule and saw me through all the way to the finish line. I consider myself to be focused and organized, but like everyone else, I need gentle reminders that deadlines are quickly approaching and that staying the course is in my best interest!

Over the past twelve years, I have trained with mentors, read and listened to various educational books and recordings, and consulted others who also dedicate their time to this work. It is not without the guidance, friendship, and support of Chris Crouch, Jan Keller, Sue DeRoos, Bethanne Kronick, and Mary Kutheis, that I began to take serious notice as to how navigating my daily life could help to serve others. We are all on this planet to find our passion and make a difference; with their encouragement, discovering what that passion is helped define what I do as "my life's work" instead of it being "my job."

A sincere thank you to my clients; not only have you been the blessings in my life that ignite me to "change the world, one disorganized person at a time," but you continually lift me up as I hope to do the same for you. Your triumphs of determination, commitment, and success to living differently are what drive me every day to continue the coaching, motivating, and empowering that I love to do.

To Stephen H. Jones, Julie Rogers, Kelly Powley, and Vanessa Lowry, the "Team Wendy" that has come together organically and enthusiastically over the past few years. I am so grateful to have you on this journey with me and appreciate your insights, your advice, your honesty, and your faith in me, my passion, and my message. Thank you to BookLogix, for leading me through this process with professionalism, patience, and the expertise to make this the book I intend it to be.

And lastly, but most importantly, my husband Marty Ellin. It is your undying support and belief in me that enabled my discovery that what I am doing in this universe is not only a gift to those I help, but my opportunity to realize the passion and truth I was meant to live. Our partnership welcomes and encourages us both to do what makes us truly happy, fulfilled and connected to our soul's purpose. For that, and so much more that you offer me, I am profoundly grateful.

Any thought telling you 'it can't be done' is only as convincing as you're willing to be held captive by its lie. Getting started—with whatever it may be—is as simple as remembering that there's nothing in the universe that can stop you from taking the first step.

Guy Finley

Go to
www.wendyellin.com/bookdownloads
to order your
Command Central tools.

WENDY ELLIN